Skeleton American

& Other Poems

Joe Maldonado

Skeleton American

Copyright © 2020 by Joe Maldonado

15 Day Poetry Chapbook Challenge

www.localgemspoetrypress.com

Table of Contents

Skeleton American

A noise is coming from the closet
of our star-spangled home
beyond the Kardashian clatter
beneath the whirring of the drones
It's so simple to hear
what our fore-bearers intone
just pull out your ear buds
put down the phone
ignore the talking head chatter
and the roar around the end zone
sounds of history abound
in a language all their own
need no Rosetta Stone to translate
the rattling of bones

First law of thermodynamics

If matter is neither destroyed or created
to where are our ephemeral cells fated?
From a blast of star particles we came
you me sun and moon
all parts of the same
we are water
we are oxygen
we are vapor
we are flame
towards infinity we fumble
eyes wide shut and breaths bated
ending where we started
crying shivering naked
From atoms to atoms
Stardust to stardust
Playing the eternal game
Of contract and combust
You me sun and moon
All parts of the same
Hurtling through space-time

To that place from which we came

The creeps

Evil doesn't yell
It whispers
Into your ear
Like a gnat
on a summer night

But evil doesn't fly
It slithers
Across the mind
Like an earthworm
after a rainy day

And yet, evil isn't wet
It shrivels
Your entire being
Like a slug
showered with salt

Much ado about tiny shoes

He turns that bright red cart
With the busted wheel
Down the wrong aisle
And his heart becomes ice
His legs turn to steel
When dangling
in his peripheral view
Is a brand new pair
Of tiny pink shoes
Like the ones
they would've wrapped up
And sat next to the balloons
And then they would've opened
To a chorus of awws and oohs
Maybe she would've worn them
For a month or two
But you know how it goes,
So big , so soon
And he's picturing her pink dress
On the first day of school

And her teenage phases
Just trying to be cool
The first date
The graduation cap
Perhaps a wedding too
His brain buzzes electric
As an almost-life passes through
His face is stone
His feet are glue
How can somebody
Never born
Be so hard to lose?

Break

Wall Street, it's time for lunch,
sky-scraping glass pillars
reflect the summer sun
Go-getters scarf down
dirty-water dogs then run
towards downtown daydreams
made of fool's gold

I sit silent
on a hot metal bench
Think "sorry, man,
it's gotten too hard to pretend"
Unravel my tie,
reach for notebook and pen,
allow my soul to explode

Paralysis in the produce section

I

Went

To buy

An apple

Seemed a simple task

But then I found myself staring

Cold and alone amidst a pile of red yellow green

Gala and golden and granny how is one supposed to
choose in times of such plenty?

Last Summer at Smith Point

The white-foam waves crashed upon the
soulless shore,
Desperate seagulls circled the salted air
in fruitless pursuit of old French fries,
And deer roamed freely upon steamy asphalt,
The pedestrian tunnels held no echoes,
Their walls untainted by freshly coated graffiti,
The drawbridge hung
motionless over the Narrow Bay
And it's waters teemed with resurgent life,
As we stood home wondering
What sounds a beach makes
with nobody there to listen

The sign on the ward door says

"Droplet precaution"
microscopic molecules,
mountainous unease

A tragedy in Anytown

Headline splatters red
Across the front page
Another young man succumbs
To the coming of rage

Not one eyeball is batted
this day and age.
What's one more bloody Sunday
In a society astray?

We'll blame the rap music,
The video games,
The Tarantino matinees,
While from the Rockies
to the Everglades,
Our young men succumb
To the coming of rage.

We've barely a moment to think or pray

So busy digging
And digging
And digging
those graves
Waiting for the next son
to succumb
To the coming of rage

Glory Days in the USA

To whom do these gilded glory days belong?
The border town babies sleeping behind steel
fences,
The CEOs stealing without fear of consequenc-
es,
The stonewalled lovers our families disowned,
The TV dad rapist we invited into our homes,
The newscaster live-streaming from the banks
of a dead river,
The Iraq war vet withering waiting for a liver,
The eight months pregnant teenage beauty
queen,
The brute flying off the top rope getting paid to
bleed,
The electric car factory worker ill from sucking
on pollution,
The cellar dweller intellectual busy building a
revolution.
Whose glory days are these if they're not our
own?

Will we look back with eyes aglow
After the next Superstorm Someone subsumes
Asbury Park?
Will you still make art
And caress my scars
When we're dancing in the dark?

It's about time

Sometimes
You will sit and think about the bad times
And wonder why they happened at all

Sometimes
you will think about the good times
and wonder why you let them slip away

Sometimes
you'll complain that there's never any time
and sometimes you'll say you've been waiting
forever

Sometimes
you'll wish for just one more time
and sometimes you'll swear
this is the last time

But there is no last time
Like there was no first time

Because the only time
You'll ever have
Is Now

Vacation

We
Used
To
Imagine
Adventures
In
Other
Worlds
Now
We
Yearn
To
Sleep
Just
One
Night
In
Another
City

21st century Nobodies

I'm nobody, who are you?
Are you nobody too?
That makes a pair of us, don't tell!
Still got our 15 minutes, let's use them well

How dreary to be somebody,
With a million-subscriber blog,
Posting thoughts the livelong day,
Only to be publicly flogged!

Harvest

That Fall you felt stuck,
did you consider your place?
Were you the tree, leaf, or breeze?

Perhaps you were an
Indian summer, holding
the heat when 'twas time to reap

The color of hope

The ancient Greeks had no word for blue
So when you're trying to start a life anew
Turn your mind's kaleidoscope askew
Watch yesterday's hazy spaces become today's
fresh hues
Your love, fire-engine red
Your fears, submarine yellow
Your dreams the fifty shades of green between
the earth and el cielo
Those once rocky gray travesties
Now purple mountain majesties
Your ambitions, illuminated indigo,
Hesitations, two-toned;
One side chartreuse, the other moonstone
Alabaster anxieties
And Rose-gold reliefs
Wine-tinged worries
Washing over you
While you lay down to sleep
And just when you reach wit's end

That culmination of your rope
you will find a beacon
The incomparable color of hope

About the Author

Joe Maldonado lives on Long Island with his wife, their dog Rya, and their cat, Leeloo Dallas Multipass. His poems can be found in various anthologies as well as his collection *Subterranean Summer*.

www.ingramcontent.com/pod-product-compliance
Lightning Source LLC
Chambersburg PA
CBHW051943150726
47999CB00006B/2342